DEVELOPING PERSONAL MASTERY

Self-coaching questions, inspiration, tips, and practical exercises for becoming an awesome manager

⌘

Managerial Competencies Series
Playbook No. 2

CÉLESTE GRIMARD

Copyright © 2018 Céleste Grimard, Canada

All rights reserved. All materials on these pages are copyrighted by Céleste Grimard. Reproduction, modification, storage of all or a part of this book in a retrieval system or retransmission, in any form or by any means, electronic, mechanical or otherwise is strictly prohibited without prior written permission from the author. Although every effort has been made to indicate the sources of text and ideas, it's possible that we missed some! If you're aware of references or citations that haven`t been provided, please be sure to contact the author. This book does not constitute legal advice and isn't a substitute for independent professional advice.
ISBN-13: 978-1979023146

CreateSpace, Charleston, SC USA

ACKNOWLEDGMENTS

I originally developed this series as a self-study, self-paced program for hundreds of managers working in a geographically dispersed area. Over the span of many years, these awesome managers offered me feedback, inspiration, and encouragement to transform this program into a series of practical, easy to read books accessible to all managers. Thank you! I also thank Rhiannon Ward for her assistance in editing and proofreading the books in this series.

CONTENTS

Series Introduction	1
Introduction	3
1. Reality Check: Self-Coaching Questions	21
2. Inspiring Your Journey	31
3. Tips for Awesome Managers	38
4. Dilemmas: What Would You Do?	67
5. Planning For Action	72
About the Managerial Competencies Series	74
References	98

DEVELOPING PERSONAL MASTERY

Welcome to the Managerial Competencies Series!

The aim of this series is to help you understand and build the core competencies you need to become an awesome manager.

There's no getting around it. There are tons of journals, books, blogs, videos – you name it – on the topic of managing. Yes, a lot has been written and said about how to be an effective manager. Everyone has their own spin to put on this topic, and research studies on this topic are practically endless. How does a busy manager sort through all the fads and fashions to find the nuggets of wisdom?

In designing this series, I pored over loads of resources and talked with hundreds of managers. I set aside all the fashions, fads, and fantasies, and I extracted only what is likely to be of enduring value to you. Although this series is

DEVELOPING PERSONAL MASTERY

geared towards practical, immediate use, I hope that it will provoke you to think deeply about managing and your role as a manager, and that it will make a difference for you so you can make a difference for others.

This module – Developing Personal Mastery – is the second of 15 books, each covering a key competency of awesome managers. **Turn to page 74 to learn more about this series**, including the full slate of books, how each book is structured, and tips on how to get the most out of them.

Throughout the book, I will refer to your **learning journal** and your **feedback team. These helpful tools are explained on pages 89 and 90.**

DEVELOPING PERSONAL MASTERY: INTRODUCTION

Awesome managers demonstrate personal mastery through responsibility, emotional resilience, constructive attitudes, self-confidence, competence, conscientiousness, and adaptability.

DEVELOPING PERSONAL MASTERY

Think about a public figure who, in your opinion, displays high levels of personal mastery, in other words, someone who "has their act together." This might be someone whose work is visible in the media, such as a politician, a businessperson, a character in a movie, etc. Now think about someone you personally know who also demonstrates personal mastery. In your learning journal, write their names and three specific things each of them do that reflect a high level of personal mastery.

Do the actions in your list fall into one or more of the following 7 categories? People who exercise personal mastery tend to:
→ **take responsibility** for their thoughts, feelings, and actions
→ be **emotionally resilient**
→ experience and express **positive attitudes**
→ have a sense of **confidence** in their skills and their value as individuals
→ continually develop their level of **competence**
→ be **conscientious** in their work

DEVELOPING PERSONAL MASTERY

→ be **adaptable**, flexible, and responsive to change.

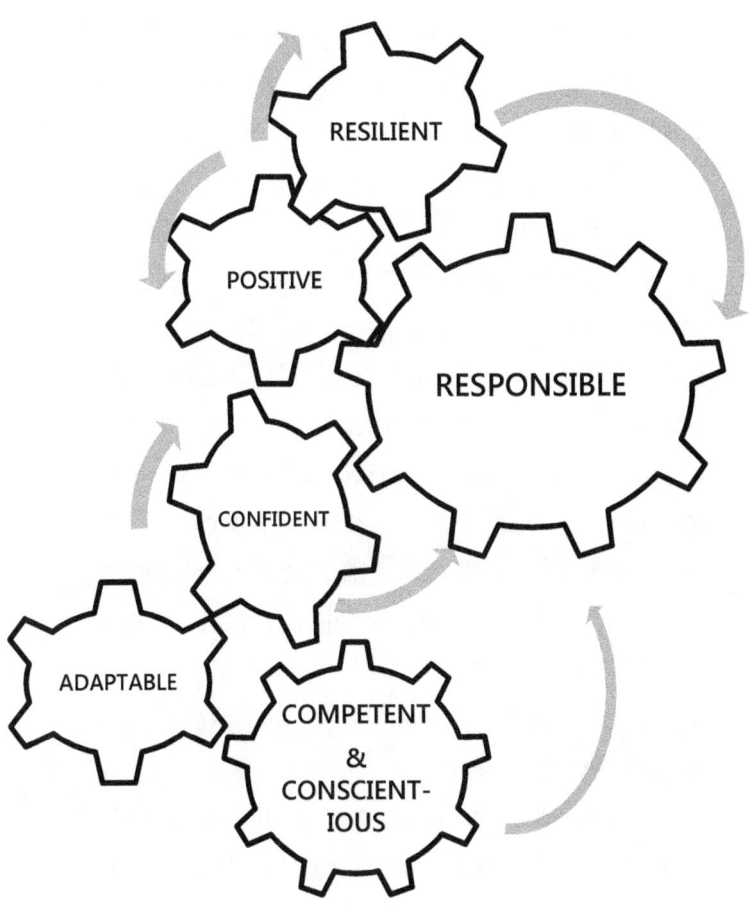

DEVELOPING PERSONAL MASTERY

Since these skills are inter-related, people who tend to take responsibility, for example, are also likely to demonstrate competency in the remaining areas of personal mastery. People who are self-confident feel in control of their destinies and adapt to changing situations. People who are confident are more likely to be perceived as competent. If you work on developing your level of competence, you may begin to feel a sense of self-efficacy or confidence, which, in turn, helps you to feel more competent. Because of all of these connections or feedback loops, working to develop one set of skills can provide you with more benefits in other areas. However, these interdependencies also mean that, if you're having difficulty with a particular area of personal mastery, other areas are likely to be negatively affected.

Let's look at each personal mastery skill separately. As you read about each skill, rate how well it describes you on a scale of 1 (not at all like me) to 10 (that's me 100%) in your learning journal.

DEVELOPING PERSONAL MASTERY

Taking Responsibility

Taking responsibility for your feelings, thoughts, and actions involves viewing yourself as the author of your life. It means having an *internal locus of control*, in other words, believing that what happens to you is caused by your skill, efforts, and actions. From your perspective, life is what you make it, and your successes and failures depend on you. Rather than blaming others, you take responsibility for your part in the events around you. You don't wait for opportunities or for others to approach you. Nope! Rather, you take personal initiative to make things happen and to repair any damaged relationships.

In contrast, people with an *external locus of control* tend to chalk things up to luck, fate, or circumstances beyond their control. These folks perceive themselves as victims of circumstances who are helpless to the forces around them. They rarely take responsibility for their results or "what happens" and don't take initiative to make things better.

DEVELOPING PERSONAL MASTERY

Research indicates that people with an external locus of control are more likely to be dissatisfied with their jobs, feel alienated from their work, and require close supervision, rigid routine and structure to be successful at work. The opposite is true for people with an internal locus of control who are more likely to be successful at work and in life in general. These folks tend to do well as managers because of their strong personal motivation and tendency to take initiative.

Being Emotionally Resilient

Emotional resilience is the ability to recognize and manage your personal emotions and others' emotions. It's the foundation of emotional intelligence, which is a cluster of abilities that people use to recognize and manage emotions in themselves and others. Awareness of your emotions is the first step to regulating or managing them. After you master control of your emotions, the next step is to develop an awareness of other people's

DEVELOPING PERSONAL MASTERY

emotions. This, in turn, serves as the foundation for building relationships with others.

People who are highly emotionally resilient can put themselves in a good mood and even motivate themselves to achieve their goals. Whether they're feeling angry, sad, or lethargic, they're able to pick themselves up. They view their emotions as a signal that what they're doing or thinking is working for them (or not). They also don't allow the negativity or rudeness of others to determine their personal emotions. Any emotions that they have are their choice and under their control.

In contrast, people with low levels of emotional resilience generally consider their emotions to be their master (rather than the opposite). They express whatever emotions they happen to feel, and they allow others' emotions to sway their own emotions. They don't try to consciously regulate their emotions for their own or others' benefit. Their mode of functioning is reactive rather than constructive.

DEVELOPING PERSONAL MASTERY

Expressing Positive Attitudes

Taking responsibility and being emotionally resilient work together to build a sense of self-control. They can help you achieve a positive attitude that is optimistic and cheerful. If you have a positive attitude, you tend to see the constructive aspects of situations. You tend to be "a ray of sunshine" or, as REO Speedwagon would say, "a candle in the window on a cold, dark winter's night." When others are negative and cynical, you maintain an upbeat and hopeful perspective on things, which is more productive and improves everyone's morale.

In contrast, people with negative attitudes tend to be cynical, sarcastic and pessimistic about circumstances in their lives. They feel frustrated and even helpless about how things are going. They commiserate, complain, and shift blame onto others rather than appreciating their own contribution to their situation. Since negativity is highly contagious, it can spread to others and bring down an entire team!

DEVELOPING PERSONAL MASTERY

Feeling Confident

Self-confidence is key to leadership. People are more likely to trust and follow managers who are confident in their own capabilities. Self-confidence tends to be rooted in a sense of self-esteem, the degree to which people see themselves as having personal worth. If you're highly self-confident, you feel secure about yourself, your knowledge, your judgment, your competence, and your actions. You admit your mistakes rather than hiding them or being defensive about them. You're decisive and able to remain calm when under pressure and in times of crisis. You see yourself as being a good person who can confidently handle the situations that you face.

According to research, people with high levels of self-esteem:
→ Expect to be successful in whatever they do
→ Believe that they can handle any challenges that come their way
→ Are more likely to choose unconventional careers

DEVELOPING PERSONAL MASTERY

→ Are more willing to take unpopular stands or positions
→ Are more assertive in dealing with external demands and pressures
→ Are more likely to be satisfied with their work
→ Are autonomous rather than dependent on others
→ Are more willing to participate in self-development activities
→ Are less likely to feel anxious in threatening situations
→ Are more likely to experience physical and mental health.

In contrast, people with low levels of self-esteem:
→ Are more vulnerable to external influences and peer pressure
→ Are more dependent on receiving positive feedback from others
→ Are more likely to conform their beliefs and behaviors to those around them and are unlikely to express dissenting opinions

DEVELOPING PERSONAL MASTERY

→ Are highly concerned with being liked by others
→ Tend to withdraw from others
→ Are usually passive in dealing with external demands and pressures
→ Are more likely to feel anxious in threatening situations
→ Are riddled with self-doubt and indecisiveness.

The idea of self-confidence presents an interesting paradox. Those who are confident in themselves tend to be humble individuals who possess quiet strength. They don't feel a need to blow their own horn or grab credit for all the good things that happen around them. They respect themselves *and* others; they don't put others down or minimize their worth and accomplishments in order to raise themselves up. They don't feel threatened by others' accomplishments; rather, they delight in them.

A lack of self-confidence can show itself in two contrasting ways: (a) through self-effacing behavior in which people think less of

DEVELOPING PERSONAL MASTERY

themselves; or (b) through self "bloating," including masking or defensive mechanisms such as arrogance, egotism, haughtiness narcissism, conceit, superiority, self-absorption, self-importance, and pomposity. People with low self-confidence tend to be unsure about what they have to offer and are reluctant to express their opinion and show leadership. Alternative, they may come across as having *excessively high* self-confidence and be overly self-focused and "full of themselves." They may think that they're right, and others are wrong.

Demonstrating Competence

Competent people have the knowledge, skills, and abilities required to do their jobs well, They are continuously developing: (a) specific skills unique to their current work; (b) skills and knowledge that can be transferred to other challenges, (c) taken for granted or unspoken knowledge about how work gets done in the organization, and (d) their networks within and outside the organization. They view themselves

DEVELOPING PERSONAL MASTERY

as "works in progress," and they believe that there is always a great deal more to learn. They are constantly looking for ways to do their work better and to improve themselves. Not only do they view challenges or difficulties as learning opportunities, but they also actively seek out the lessons to be learned from every situation. Highly competent people are committed to continuous learning and have a "thirst for knowledge."

In contrast, people with low levels of competence don't actively seek out learning opportunities and new ways of doing things. They believe that meeting the minimum demands of their role or "being good enough" is simply ... good enough. They don't challenge themselves to excel in everything they do.

Being Conscientious

Conscientious people are diligent, dependable, hardworking, responsible, perseverant, and productive. They have a strong work ethic and have probably been complimented on their

DEVELOPING PERSONAL MASTERY

self-discipline, their organizational skills, and their ability to manage their workload and rise to the challenge when faced with difficult tasks.

However, if excessive, conscientiousness can develop into perfectionism and workaholism. Perfectionists and workaholics have difficulty setting appropriate limits. Although, in the past, it was fashionable to call yourself a perfectionist or a workaholic, both have since been recognized as dysfunctional patterns of behavior. They are rooted in self-doubt and a need to prove yourself. Both of these can lead to strained work and personal relationships as well as poor health.

Perfectionists:

→ Compulsively set extremely high standards for themselves and others
→ Obsess and become overwhelmed by task details while ignoring the overall purpose of the task
→ Are overly critical of themselves and others
→ Are disappointed when they receive less than perfect evaluations

DEVELOPING PERSONAL MASTERY

→ Never feel that they or their work measure up.

Workaholics:

→ Are highly involved in and committed to their work
→ Are anxious and potentially compulsive about their work
→ Have trouble relaxing and not thinking about or doing work
→ Regularly allow work concerns and tasks to overflow into family or leisure time
→ Have difficulty maintaining reasonable boundaries between work and the rest of their lives
→ Define themselves in terms of their jobs and their success at work.

For their part, people who are low in conscientiousness tend to be unreliable, lazy, easily sidetracked and distracted, impulsive, careless, and prone to making excuses. They wait till the last minute to accomplish a task and, as a result, do it poorly. They tend to have trouble paying attention to detail, being

DEVELOPING PERSONAL MASTERY

dependable, organizing themselves, and persisting when tasks become challenging. Others may view them as slackers or, in group situations, freeloaders who depend on others to do the work.

Extensive research has found that conscientiousness is the single most important predictor of success and health in life and at work. As you can imagine, awesome managers are conscientious folks.

Demonstrating Adaptability

Adaptable people are comfortable with ambiguity and uncertainty, are open to change, and are able to adjust to situational and individual demands. When presented with new information that challenges their existing views or "mental maps," they re-examine their assumptions. Adaptable people are willing to forego what they have traditionally done, step outside of what is comfortable to them (their comfort zone), and tailor their actions to the needs of the situation and the people involved.

DEVELOPING PERSONAL MASTERY

In contrast, people who have trouble adapting tend to stubbornly and rigidly hold on to their opinions and ways of doing things. For them, it's "their way or the highway." They may believe that there's only one right way to do things or view a situation, and that happens to be their way! They resist change and are inflexible in dealing with situations and people.

Managers need to be adaptable:

→ In responding to or leading organizational change. If organizational priorities shift, adaptable managers "roll with the punches" and make any adjustments that are needed. This is especially important given the pace of change in today's organizations and society as a whole. Managers who resist change and seek to protect the status quo serve as poor role models for employees.

→ In working with employees from diverse backgrounds, ages, personalities, and views of how work should be done. Often, there are many different ways to accomplish a task. Managers need to be open to listening to what employees have to say

DEVELOPING PERSONAL MASTERY

and to experimenting with these different approaches.
→ In responding to situational demands. Managers need to adapt how they manage employees given differences in their levels of commitment and competency in performing particular tasks.

The balancing point between rigidity (being "stuck in the mud") and impulsiveness is adaptability. It's a judgment call that managers must make. Whereas rigid people stick to one course of action or opinion regardless of the need for change, impulsive people are too eager to devalue and discard the past in favor of change, regardless of its necessity or potential impact. They act without thinking things through, and they jump onto whatever bandwagon that is passing through. As a result, their employees tend to view them and their decisions as unpredictable.

DEVELOPING PERSONAL MASTERY

1

REALITY CHECK: SELF COACHING QUESTIONS

To help you examine your personal mastery, we invite you to ask yourself a series of self-coaching questions and record your answers in your learning journal. While thinking about your behavior in the past six months or so, find specific examples that support your answers. Consider whether or not "counter examples" exist; in other words, times when you may not

DEVELOPING PERSONAL MASTERY

have behaved in a manner that is consistent with your answer. In answering these questions, think about how you generally are rather than temporary aberrations due to stress or other factors.

Your answers to these self-coaching questions will shine a light on how you see yourself. If you know yourself well, your answers will be right on the mark. However, many people don't have entirely accurate self-perceptions, either because they're not used to assessing themselves or because they feel uncomfortable with the idea of reflecting on their own behaviors. As a result, their answers may be *extreme*: either inflated or very low.

In all cases, but especially when answers are extreme (in any direction), seeking candid and honest feedback from others can be a valuable means of shedding light on your actual competency levels. In other words, you can learn a lot more about yourself if you get feedback from others. You can do so by asking them to answer some of the self-coaching questions for you.

DEVELOPING PERSONAL MASTERY

They may not tell you what you want to hear, but it may be exactly what you need to help you make progress on your journey toward becoming an awesome manager. As American writer Herbert Sebastian Aga said in his book *A Time for Greatness*, "the truth that makes men free is, for the most part, the truth which men prefer not to hear." Asking others for feedback takes courage on everyone's part. Others don't necessarily have the same picture of you as you have of yourself, and people are sometimes reluctant to "tell it like it is." However, "feedback-lite" that is polite and tells you what you hope to hear won't help you grow as a person. Tell people that you need the straight goods (politely though!).

Do I take responsibility?

→ How responsible do I believe I am for what happens to me?
→ Do I explain positive events in my career and life with a sense of pride in my accomplishments? Or do I have a "I was at the right place at the right time" attitude (suggesting that they were due to luck)?
→ Do I assume responsibility for difficult decisions? Or, do I tend to make excuses or shift responsibility unto others?
→ When I screw up, do I admit it?
→ Do I take initiative to resolve any relationship issues that I have with others? Or, do I wait for others to make the first move?

Am I emotionally resilient?

→ Do I feel in control of myself most of the time? Or do I sometimes feel helpless or overwhelmed by my circumstances?
→ Am I a calm, collected person? Or do I tend to feel anxious or lose my temper?

DEVELOPING PERSONAL MASTERY

→ Can I keep my cool during a traffic jam? Or do I feel impatient and frustrated?
→ When I feel anxious, can I usually calm myself down?
→ How do I motivate myself to accomplish my goals?
→ When I'm feeling down, can I usually pick myself up?
→ Is my mood always in my own control or do I allow the negativity of people around me to infect my mood?
→ When people are rude to me, do I take it in stride? Or am I rude in return?
→ Would others say that I am optimistic? Or would they say that I worry a lot?

Am I in control of my attitude?

→ What would my boss say about my attitude? Is it usually positive? Negative?
→ Do I tend to see the glass as half full? Or half empty? Or not at all?
→ Overall, am I a happy person?
→ Do I view challenges as opportunities?
→ Would others say that I'm a trusting

person? Or suspicious and cynical?
- → Do I feel positive about my future? Or do I generally feel frustrated about how things are going in my life?
- → Do I expect the best outcomes? Or the worst outcomes? How often are my expectations justified?

Am I confident?

- → Do I have a healthy level of self-esteem? Or do I enjoy talking about myself way too much? Or too little?
- → How do I feel about my abilities as a manager?
- → Can I generally handle anything that's put on my plate at work?
- → How do I feel about who I am as a person?
- → Would others say I display humility?
- → Do I believe that everyone has their strengths and weaknesses? Or do I believe that I am, on average, smarter or better than most people?
- → Do I believe in the common good? Or do I believe in "looking out for number one"

(me!) first and foremost?
→ Am I willing to admit when I'm wrong? Or do I have a strong need to be right?

Am I competent?

→ In the past year, have others complimented me on my level of job competence?
→ Do I seek out opportunities to discuss ideas with people? How can I do more of this?
→ Do I have good overall life skills? How well am I taking charge of and managing my life responsibilities?
→ Do I feel like I'm constantly learning from the people around me?
→ Would my employees say that I'm a good manager?
→ Do I feel comfortable in my capabilities at work? Or do I often doubt my ability to do at least part of my job?
→ Do my colleagues and/or managers generally trust my capabilities? Or has my ability to do at least part of my job been questioned in the past year?
→ Do I have a thirst for learning new things?

Am I conscientious?

- → Would others say that I'm dependable?
- → How much effort and thought do I generally put into my work?
- → Am I hard-working? Or do I do the minimum needed to get by?
- → How's my self-discipline?
- → Am I an organized person? Or have I been told I need to be more organized?
- → Do I pay attention to detail? Or do I need to pay closer attention to details?
- → Do I persevere when something is challenging? Or, when things get hard or take too long, do I quit or expect reduced standards?
- → Do I have a balanced perspective of the place of work in my life? Or do I have perfectionist or workaholic tendencies?

Am I flexible and adaptable?

- → How easily do I adapt to a change of plans?
- → Do I adjust to differences in situational demands or differences in how others work

DEVELOPING PERSONAL MASTERY

without difficulty?
- → Would others say that I tend to be accommodating to others' needs? Or do I tend to be stubborn and insist that we do things MY WAY (because I know the best way to do things, of course)?
- → Do I let others make decisions and work in their own ways (as long as it's within my workplace's policies)? Or do I have a need to control and micromanage everything that happens in my work unit?
- → Do I find that others can do things as well as I would do them (or better)?
- → Do I try new things? Or would others say that I'm inflexible or stuck in my ways?
- → Am I generally open to hearing what others have to say? Do I make an effort to understand others' points of view? When was the last time that I significantly changed my way of thinking about something or someone? Or do I have a fixed mindset that says that people can't change much, if at all?

Reflection

What do your answers say about what you consider to be your strengths and your opportunities for improvement in relation to personal mastery? Do you feel in control of yourself, your actions, emotions, and attitudes? Are you self-assured and flexible? Or do you need to work on your levels of confidence and adaptability?

What feedback did others give you about these aspects of yourself? Did their answers and yours overlap? If not, why might this be the case?

These can be tough questions to face. They may have brought up memories of moments you aren't proud of, or things you know you could develop. The important point here is feeling motivated to work on improving yourself, not punishing yourself for having less than *perfect* answers.

2

INSPIRING YOUR JOURNEY

As you read through the following quotations, take note of the ones that speak to you the most. Then consider the message they are conveying to you.

DEVELOPING PERSONAL MASTERY

He that would govern others first should be the master of himself.
Philip Massigner

⌘

We are our own raw material. Only when we know what we're made of and what we want to make of it can we begin our lives.
Warren Bennis

⌘

You make your life your own by understanding it. Self-awareness = self-knowledge = self-possession = self-control = self-expression.
Warren Bennis

⌘

No man thinks there is much ado about nothing when the ado is about himself.
Anthony Trollope

⌘

A person himself is very much what he thinks of others.
Lawrence Lovasik

DEVELOPING PERSONAL MASTERY

If our definition or concept of ourselves comes from what others think of us – from the social mirror – we will gear our lives to their wants and their expectations; and the more we live to meet the expectations of others, the more weak, shallow, and insecure we become.
Stephen Covey

⌘

Instead of condemning people, try to understand them. Any fool can criticize, condemn, and complain – and most fools do. But it takes character and self-control to be understanding and forgiving.
Lawrence Lovasik

⌘

Everything can be taken from a man but one thing: the last of the human freedoms – to choose one's attitude in any given set of circumstances.
Victor Frankl

⌘

Life is a long lesson in humility.
James M. Barrie

DEVELOPING PERSONAL MASTERY

No one can make you feel inferior without your consent.
Eleanor Roosevelt

⌘

We are free to choose our response in any situation but, in doing do, we choose the attendant consequences … It is not what others do or even our own mistakes that hurts us the most; it is our response to those things.
Stephen Covey

⌘

It is easy to blame others. It takes courage to hold ourselves responsible for the difficulties we face. It is rare and shocking to hear someone say, "I missed the schedule because I did not manage the project well."
Peter Block

⌘

You cannot always control circumstances, but you can control your own thoughts.
Charles Popplestown

DEVELOPING PERSONAL MASTERY

What I see without is a reflection of what I have first seen within my own mind. I always project onto the world the thoughts, feelings, and attitudes which preoccupy me. I can see the world differently only by changing my mind about what I want to see.
Gerald Jampolsky

⌘

Many people believe that humility is the opposite of pride, when, in fact, it is a point of equilibrium. The opposite of pride is actually a lack of self-esteem. A humble person is totally different from a person who cannot recognize and appreciate himself as part of this world's marvels.
Rabino Nilton Bonder

⌘

Pride is concerned with who is right. Humility is concerned with what is right.
Ezra Taft Benson

DEVELOPING PERSONAL MASTERY

Taking responsibility means recognizing that, at every moment, you are free to choose to think certain thoughts, feel certain emotions, and do whatever it is that you're doing. An average day is filled with hundreds of opportunities to make such choices. You are accountable for both what you do and what you don't do and any consequences of your actions and non-actions regardless of pressure from those around you to compromise the fabric of your conscience. Responsible people stand behind their decisions and non-decisions rather than shifting the blame onto other individuals or the circumstances. Responsible people recognize their "complicity in the triumph of evil" when nothing is done to stop it.

www.charactercounts.org

DEVELOPING PERSONAL MASTERY

We are not born with maps; we have to make them, and the making requires effort. The more effort we make to appreciate and perceive reality, the larger and more accurate our maps will be. But many do not want to make this effort. Their maps are small and sketchy, their views of the world narrow and misleading.
M. Scott Peck

What are your five favorite quotations?

Why do these stand out for you?

Which would you want to adopt as your personal motto? Include on the signature line of your emails? Post on your desk?

3

TIPS FOR AWESOME MANAGERS

As you review the following list of actions that you can take to develop personal mastery, circle, check or highlight those that are especially meaningful for you.

DEVELOPING PERSONAL MASTERY

1. **Take initiative to do what needs to be done** rather than saying "it's not my job."

2. **Take initiative to repair damaged relationships** rather than waiting for the other person to make the first move.

3. **Take responsibility** for your successes and failures; say "I'm choosing to do this" not "this is happening to me." Focus on what you can do, not what isn't possible.

4. **Focus on fixing problems rather than assigning blame.** Try to not make any excuses or rationalizations for an entire week, both at work and at home. See how often you tend to do both and in which circumstances. This experiment can help you identify how much of what you say and think consists of excuses or blaming others.

DEVELOPING PERSONAL MASTERY

5. **Avoid "us versus them" thinking.** Try to find objectives that you have in common.

6. **Avoid playing the following common games** (adapted from Stephen Karpman's Drama Triangle theory).
   → **Kick Me**: setting yourself up for punishment or criticism by not meeting expectations or deadlines.
   → **If It Weren't For You**: blaming your poor results or failures on external causes.
   → **Yes, But...**: attempting to appear reasonable but actually remaining closed to others' opinions.
   → **I've Got Too Much To Do**: taking on a heavy workload as a way of justifying not doing anything very well.
   → **There IS No Way Out, So What Can You Do?**: giving up and not doing anything out of a sense of helplessness.
   → **Let Me Help You**: helping others who may not even need or want the help.

DEVELOPING PERSONAL MASTERY

- → **You're Fine Except For**: disparaging others by focusing on one of their minor (negative) characteristics.
- → **Now I've Got You, You SOB**: waiting for someone to make a mistake and then pouncing on them.

7. **Consider whether or not you're playing games** in your relationships with others. If so, ask yourself the following questions:
   - → What do I want this relationship to be like?
   - → How can I express my point of view in a more direct and considerate manner?

8. **Review your experiences** over the past 6 months and identify those times when you assumed the role of a victim (blaming others, feeling persecuted, not feeling in control of a situation, looking for someone to rescue you). Think of a more appropriate non-victim response for those situations.

DEVELOPING PERSONAL MASTERY

9. **In addition to avoiding the victim role, beware of the "persecutor" role** (blaming, nitpicking and criticizing; being rigid, bossy and authoritarian) **and the "rescuer" role** (feeling guilty if you don't help victims in some way, keeping victims dependent and giving them permission to fail, frequently advising others or giving your opinion about what they should do). These three roles make up Stephen Karpman's Drama Triangle. He says that all of these roles are unhealthy and to be avoided. A first step is becoming aware of the roles you tend to play. The next step is to "move off the triangle" (not play any role) and deal with people in a straight-forward manner.

10. **Be aware when a drama triangle is forming and don't accept invitations to hop on.** It usually starts with a person feeling victimized and pointing fingers at their apparent persecutor and then looking for a rescuer. Refuse to intervene if it's not in

DEVELOPING PERSONAL MASTERY

your area of responsibility, capability, or interest.

11. **Don't play manipulative games.** Be honest, direct, open, and specific. Don't correct others' statements about how they feel. Don't tell them how they should or shouldn't feel. Rather, try to understand why they feel this way, and acknowledge their feelings.

12. **Develop a more mature outlook on life.** According to Stephen Covey, people grow in maturity as they move from being dependent on others ("It's *your* responsibility to take care of me") to independence ("*I'm* in charge of my life") to interdependence ("*We* can make things happen together"). Victims and rescuers tend to be stuck in a state of dependence, while persecutors are likely to be counter-dependent. In contrast to independent folks who have an "approach" mindset,

DEVELOPING PERSONAL MASTERY

counter-dependent people have an "avoidance" self-protective mindset.

13. Recognize that every day is full of decisions, and **you are accountable for both what you do *and* what you don't do.**

14. **Stay in the here and now** and cope with reality. If you blame others or the world for your problems, or if your behavior is aimed at making yourself simply *feel better* instead of solving your problems, you are ensuring that the status quo will continue.

15. **Decide who, how, and what you want to be** without making excuses, justifying, blaming, or repeatedly saying "I'm sorry."

16. **Don't demand perfection from yourself and others**. Set realistic goals that you want to achieve. Recognize feelings of inadequacy and guilt as legacies from your past. Guilt is productive when it signals that we have done something inappropriate. But, we

need to address this feeling and then move on.

17. **Refuse to be manipulated** by other people's greed, helplessness, or anger. Set limits. Say "no" when you mean "no." Confront those who try to manipulate you by telling you what you should or shouldn't do and how to live your life.

18. **Identify the emotions that you're experiencing at any given moment.** Go beyond recognizing that you're feeling good, bad or so-so. Although Paul Ekman's extensive research found that six basic emotions (anger, fear, sadness, happiness, surprise, and disgust) are universally expressed and recognized, many combinations of these emotions exist. People often feel several emotions at the same time (for example, being afraid and sad). Understanding the specific emotions that you're feeling may help you determine what caused or triggered those emotions.

DEVELOPING PERSONAL MASTERY

Recognizing your emotions and their triggers will help you build your level of emotional control and resilience.

19. **Accept your emotions.** Don't ignore or deny them. Share your emotions (for example, "I'm feeling confused about...") so that there is a match between what you're experiencing and expressing.

20. **Be constructively selfish.** Remember that no matter what you do, someone isn't going to like it. If you wait for everyone's approval before doing something, you'll be waiting for a very long time.

21. **Don't ask questions that you wouldn't want to answer yourself.** Depending on the nature of your relationship with another person, some questions, such as "why" or "why not" questions, come across as intrusive or potentially manipulative.

DEVELOPING PERSONAL MASTERY

22. **Practice delaying gratification.** This involves resisting temptation especially when it's a distraction or hindrance to your work and accomplishing longer-term goals. Sure, watching TV every evening may feel good in the moment, but it will get in the way of your accomplishing important goals. Don't sacrifice your goals for "feeling good" now. Try to exercise self-discipline, show responsibility and set a good example for others. Think about the long term benefits of resisting temptations!

23. **Practice tolerating frustration.** People who can tolerate frustration are able to persevere in the face of competing (and more attractive) demands. Blasting the horn and yelling at other drivers while in a traffic jam is obviously less effective than staying calm. Think about areas where tolerating frustration is challenging for you, and brainstorm some constructive alternatives.

DEVELOPING PERSONAL MASTERY

24. **Listen empathetically to others.** Stop yourself from working on counter-arguments while another person is speaking. Take the risk of being persuaded. Try the other person's reasoning on for size. Do they have a good point?

25. **Don't make assumptions** about how others think or feel or how they may react. You can't get inside anyone's head but your own. Avoid mind reading: don't presume that you know what someone else is thinking. Ask them! Don't ass-u-me that someone knows or *should* know what you want or need. Tell them!

26. **Politely confront what you consider to be corrosive or manipulative behavior** such as sarcasm, put-downs, and indirect attacks. Don't attack others in a game of "tit for tat." Revenge may be a "dish best served cold," but it only generates more revenge. Instead, ask for clarification ("I'm not sure I

DEVELOPING PERSONAL MASTERY

understood correctly. What did you mean by this?") and appeal to common goals.

27. **Think before you speak or act**. The ability to think before acting instead of blurting something out on impulse or acting out of frustration prevents mistakes or outbursts that damage relationships and result in regrets later on. Before responding impulsively, take some time to think about what's best in a particular situation. Don't be afraid to say "let me think about this." Just remember to return to the conversation in a reasonable time frame.

28. **Channel anger into solving a problem or changing a situation.** Aggressive behavior leads to regret, resentment, or problem escalation. And don't constantly suppress your emotions; this creates a time bomb that is likely to explode at a really bad moment. Remain calm, courteous, and professional. It may help to take some deep

DEVELOPING PERSONAL MASTERY

breaths, a long drink of water, or even a walk around the block.

29. **List all the negative and pessimistic views that you hold** about a particular situation. Then, try to reframe your views so that you have some positive statements to make about the situation. For at least a week, practice reframing negatives into positives, and see how well it works for you.

30. Identify a particular situation in which you feel powerless or helpless. Now consider aspects of that situation over which you do have some control (for example, your thoughts, feelings, and behaviors) and **develop a plan to build your sense of control** in that situation.

31. **Be tentative.** Don't state your opinions or interpretations as facts etched in stone, avoid preaching words, don't exaggerate, and don't bulldoze others. Avoid absolute statements that leave no room for

modification. "I think this is a good way..." is better than "This is the only way..." Give people room to maneuver and save face.

32. **Avoid being negative.** Notice when you are using words like "but," "problem," "I have to," "I can't," and "threat." Try instead to be more positive, using: "and," "opportunity," "I want to," "I can do this," and "opening." Being negative drags you and others down into a pit of despair. Being positive creates possibilities for change. Don't reject positive experiences, and don't dwell on isolated negative details.

33. **Avoid all or nothing thinking;** for example, thinking that, if your performance or results weren't perfect, then it was a total failure. Try to appreciate both the positive and negative aspects of situations. Realize that no one is perfect, and, just like everyone else, you're still learning!

DEVELOPING PERSONAL MASTERY

34. **Don't overgeneralize, jump to conclusions, or exaggerate the significance of things.** One failure doesn't make your life a failure. Get information from a variety of perspectives, and consider the situation fairly. Don't only look for opinions that support yours. Instead, deliberately seek out differing points of view.

35. **Avoid emotional reasoning.** According to David Burns, this involves assuming that your emotions reflect the way things really are: "I feel it, therefore, it must be true." Consider the facts of a situation and whether they support your feelings.

36. **Try to look in on a situation from the outside,** like a fly on the wall. Look down and watch the action, hear the dialogue, and see the process as an impartial observer instead of an integral part of the event. This can offer you a new, clear vision of the situation.

DEVELOPING PERSONAL MASTERY

37. **Ask for other people's perspectives** on a situation. Sometimes we're too close to it, and our perspective is distorted. We can't see all the possible aspects, risks, and potential of a situation.

38. **Put things in perspective.** Some things may seem important in the short-term, but are truly insignificant in the long-term. In part, this requires an appreciation that there are things that we can control and act on and things that we can't control and shouldn't act on. Follow the teachings of Serenity Prayer: "Grant me the serenity to accept the things I cannot change, the courage to change the things I can, and the wisdom to know the difference."

39. **Pay attention to the warning signs that point to a need for emotional self-control.** According to R.R. Luhn, a specialist in managing anger, these might include the following:

DEVELOPING PERSONAL MASTERY

- → **Emotional Outbursts:** Negative drama makes others feel helpless, manipulated and drained. If you have a temper, consider practicing relaxation and meditation techniques.
- → **Labeling:** Negative labels (for example, "You're lazy, incompetent, and stupid!") hurt others and spawn anger that is expressed later on. Labels are for jars, not people! Focus on behaviors, instead.
- → **Complaining:** Resist dumping on others. Constant complaining and negatively build resentment, anger, and avoidance.
- → **Indifference:** You're indifferent when you don't respond verbally or walk away when the other person is talking, when you ignore something of importance, or when you change the subject when the other person is still talking.
- → **Giving Commands:** Requests work better than orders. A simple "please" and "thank you" can go a long way.
- → **Pretending:** Pretending to be happy or to like something and pretending you're

DEVELOPING PERSONAL MASTERY

not upset when you are don't help you build solid relationships. The truth usually comes out sooner or later.

40. **Consider whether you possess "dark-side traits" that result in career derailment** (according to leadership researchers Richard Hughes and his colleagues):
→ Being argumentative and overly sensitive to criticism
→ Being interpersonally insensitive and unaware of how you're coming across
→ Being narcissistic, self-centered, arrogant, and entitlement-oriented
→ Being overly cautious due to a fear of failure
→ Micromanaging and nitpicking
→ Being self-focused at the expense of others (for example, not paying attention to the impact of what you say and do on others, not keeping promises)

DEVELOPING PERSONAL MASTERY

41. **Practice clearing**:
    → During an entire week, at the end of each day, take 10 minutes to make a list of events that were especially pleasant and enjoyable ("completes") and events in which there were leftover feelings, nagging doubts, unspoken words, or unfinished tasks ("incompletes"). Next, develop a plan to address any of the "incompletes."
    → For three weeks, prepare clearing sheets (see next page) and practice clearing at the end of each "event" or "encounter." In other words, "complete" each event or make a plan to do so before you go on. If you do this, your daily clearing sheet will only have "completes" on it.
    → After three weeks, continue to practice "on-the-spot" clearing but only prepare clearing sheets once per week.

DEVELOPING PERSONAL MASTERY

Sample Clearing Work Sheet

Problem, Thought, Positive Event	Complete	Incomplete	Plan
1. Slept in and late for work		✓	Set alarm
2. Received a letter from happy client	✓		
3. Talked to Pat about new training program		✓	Register Pat for program tomorrow
4. Lunch with Chris – had a nice talk	✓		
5. Received MasterCard bill containing extra charges		✓	Call MasterCard tomorrow about the charges
6. Games night with family	✓		

DEVELOPING PERSONAL MASTERY

42. **Practice cognitive restructuring**: It might seem like feelings *just happen*, but, according to Albert Ellis' A-B-C model, you have the ability to steer them. Point A is the activating event; for example, your boss reprimands you for not completing a project on time. Following this, you feel upset about your work performance, you become defensive, and you say, "There's only so much I can do!" (Point C). People sometimes think that the event (A) leads directly to the feelings and behavior (C). However, in between A and C is B, our thoughts. It is our thoughts that influence our feelings and behavior:

   A. Activating Event
   Reprimand from boss
   B. Your Thinking
   "I forgot all about it. I'm so stupid."
   C. Feelings and Behaviors
   Upset, defensive, yelling at others

   Although your boss got the process rolling, it's your own thinking that produced your feelings. That's why it's important to

DEVELOPING PERSONAL MASTERY

develop effective thinking habits. An event can be perceived in a variety of ways and can result in different emotional responses. In other words, it's not the event that makes you feel anything, but how you think about the event. Getting back to our example, an alternative approach would be:

A. Activating Event
Reprimand from boss
B. Your Thinking
"I wish I had finished on time, but I didn't."
C. Feelings and Behavior
Disappointment, but kept in perspective

43. **Keep a schedule** others can rely on. Being predictable reduces uncertainty and stress for others. Reliability = trustworthiness

44. **Take a day off when needed.** Chantal Binet, management coach, suggests that people take a break during every change of season; in other words, four times a year. However, day long micro-vacations are also

a good idea. They can temporarily relieve stress and improve your sense of wellness.

45. **Practice thought-stopping.** As suggested by J. Robinson, thought-stopping begins by listing six arguments that contradict the *worry* that you have. For example, if you're worrying about losing your job, you might write: (1) I have a good work record; (2) I had other job worries before that didn't materialize; (3) When out of work in the past, I succeeded in landing a job; (4) I have marketable skills; and so on. Here are the next steps:

   a. Choose a "distraction prop" such as a cup or picture.
   b. Choose a quiet time and place, sit in a comfortable chair, and relax.
   c. Deliberately bring on the disturbing thought.
   d. Once it has formed in your mind, shout the word "stop" in a commanding voice and, at the same time, slap a table or a chair. It might help to form a mental

DEVELOPING PERSONAL MASTERY

    stop-image such as a red light or a stop sign as you say the word "stop."

e. After you say "stop", immediately look at the distraction prop and say something that contradicts your worry.

f. If you still feel a bit tense, say "relax," "quiet," or "this too shall pass."

g. Repeat these steps as soon as you're aware of a disturbing thought. With practice, you'll need fewer repetitions.

46. **Exercise self-control and self-respect** by maintaining a set of personal standards of excellence. Honor your commitments to yourself, and it'll be easier to honor your commitments to others.

47. **Manage your worries**: Stephen Covey suggests that you start by making a list of the specific things that you worry about. Then, sort the problems into two groups: problems over which you have SOME control (your Circle of Influence) and problems over which you have NO control

DEVELOPING PERSONAL MASTERY

(your Circle of Concern). While reactive people exert futile effort in trying to manage their Circle of Concern, proactive people focus on enlarging their Circle of Influence. They try to find the "piece" of the situation over which they do have control even though it may seem limited. They develop an action plan for each problem in their Circle of Influence by answering the following questions:

a. What resources do I need to solve this problem?
b. Who can help me with this problem?
c. What can I do today to resolve the problem? Tomorrow?

Stephen Covey suggests that you attack problems one at a time, beginning with the easiest one. Your success with the easiest problem will boost your confidence as you move to the next problem. After doing all you can, let go and trust that things will work out.

DEVELOPING PERSONAL MASTERY

48. **Know yourself and your limits.** Don't accept more challenges than you can handle. It can be hard to say "no," but awesome managers are able to do so and delegate when helpful. Saying "no" is better than doing a poor job or not meeting deadlines.

49. **Get help when things are getting out of control.** When people feel physically ill, they see a doctor. In the same way, you should feel comfortable getting help if you're 'under the weather' psychologically or emotionally.

50. **Avoid being a sleaze, a whiner, or a slacker.** As ethics researcher Doug Chismar suggests, "Professionals treat other people as if they really mattered, rather than as tools, or mere opportunities for profit, labor, or resume-building." Don't "go off" on others or rely on intimidation to make up for feeling powerless. Likewise, don't engage in harassment (sexual or otherwise). This disrespectful behavior creates a hostile

DEVELOPING PERSONAL MASTERY

work environment for everyone, which reduces performance and job commitment.

51. **Avoid spending any part of the workday cruising inappropriate or non-work-related websites** such as porn, sports, gambling, etc. Not only will you lose the respect of others, but you can lose your job by engaging in this 'time theft.'

52. **Evaluate and reconsider any workaholic tendencies that you may have.** Spending most of your waking time working or thinking about work and feeling a compulsion or sense of anxiety about working is unhealthy. It has a serious negative impact on your family and other relationships as well as your health. And don't expect others to be compulsively driven to work. Just because you're unable to achieve balance in your life, it doesn't mean that others shouldn't. After all, we're human *beings*, not human *doings*. Do you work to live, or do you live to work?"

DEVELOPING PERSONAL MASTERY

53. **Avoid inflicting your dissatisfaction with your present job or life situation on others.** If you're unhappy, you need to do something about it: fight (try to change your situation), flight (get out of the situation), or flow (find a way to make peace with your situation).

54. **Set a goal to engage in continuous learning.** Set aside and use a block of time to access library resources, attend free lectures and seminars, listen to podcasts and educational videos, and review work-related journals and other materials. Continuous self-development is key to personal and professional growth.

55. **Become quietly effective.** Motivational guru William Dyer recommends resisting the temptation to feel that you MUST announce your victories (and defeats) to those around you. He suggests that you be your own judge instead of seeking reinforcement and affirmation from others.

DEVELOPING PERSONAL MASTERY

56. **Learn from others.** As suggested by Richard Hughes and his colleagues, we can learn by observing the behaviors and asking questions of anyone who effectively models personal mastery competencies. People are usually quite happy to share their tips and tricks.

57. **Take a "10% stretch."** In their research, Richard Hughes and his colleagues found that the difference between average and exceptional performers is usually about 10%. So, in trying to develop each of your personal mastery competencies, extend your behaviors 10% beyond your comfort zone. Small, conscious changes to your routine can have a big impact.

Now that you have read these tips, review the ones that you have circled, checked, or highlighted. What do they have in common?

DEVELOPING PERSONAL MASTERY

4

DILEMMAS: WHAT WOULD YOU DO?

This section gives you the opportunity to consider how to apply what you just learned in a sampling of situations about Sandra, a recently promoted call center manager who is struggling to cope with her new role. For each dilemma, read the situation, select the best alternative (or create your own), and explain why you consider this option to be the most appropriate solution.

DEVELOPING PERSONAL MASTERY

Situation 1: Sandra is exhausted all the time. While she can't *physically* take most of her work home with her, she does so *psychologically* every night. When she's with her family, all she can think or talk about are work problems. She's constantly checking her emails and messages. She even sneaks her cell phone into the bathroom with her. She's not sure she can keep going on this way. How can she move forward?

a. Bring home some paperwork; might as well get some work done if it's all she's going to think about!

b. Vent constantly to her family and friends – that's what they're there for!

c. Reduce her work responsibilities and avoid time-consuming tasks to make more room for her personal life.

d. Develop a set of rules for home time (for example, turning off her work phone, etc.), begin scheduling her non-work time (blocks of time for family, exercise, and more), and work on developing healthy coping strategies.

DEVELOPING PERSONAL MASTERY

Situation 2: Sandra worked in a call center for six years before becoming its manager last year. Before her promotion, the employees were her friendly and competent colleagues. But now, Sandra thinks that they have changed. They refuse to follow the new procedures that she introduced, and they seem to have a poor work ethic. In fact, last week, no one agreed to work overtime and, as a result, some shifts were short-staffed. How should she address this?

a. Cover some of the shifts herself, and let the others go short-staffed.
b. Reprimand her staff, and start scheduling mandatory overtime shifts. They should respect her policies or leave!
c. Schedule a series of one-on-one meetings with staff along with a staff meeting to ask for suggestions about how to resolve the work situation constructively.
d. Complain to her manager about her lazy employees.

DEVELOPING PERSONAL MASTERY

Situation 3: Sandra is frustrated about having inherited a group of employees who, in her opinion, seem to have nothing better to do than to complain about their schedules, their workloads, their customers, each other – and her. "Why me?" Sandra asks herself, "Just my luck to have this group of underachievers. They're making me look bad. They should respect me, but they seem to despise me." How can she move forward?

a. Tell her staff that she can't possibly deal with all of their complaints, and that there's nothing she can do about the chronic understaffing or anything else. "It's an organizational problem; not hers!"

b. At a staff meeting, admit her part in the unit's morale problem, and ask for their help in improving the work climate.

c. "Bite back" when staff complain, with remarks like "You need an attitude adjustment."

d. Figure out who might be the instigators of the problem and reprimand them.

DEVELOPING PERSONAL MASTERY

Situation 4: Sandra has discovered over time that there are many things about her job that she doesn't quite understand. As an employee, she developed excellent skills in resolving customer issues and felt competent and secure. But as a manager, Sandra has multiple procedures to follow, work schedules to develop, and meetings to attend. She isn't sure if she's doing everything she should be doing, or if she's doing it correctly. There's even some paperwork hidden in her bottom drawer. What should she do?

a. Straight out ask her boss for help.
b. Take a block of time to reflect on her work – what's working and what isn't, identify potential solutions for addressing the gaps, and develop a plan. Then, she should work out a final plan with her boss.
c. Realize that it's too late to ask her boss questions that she should already know the answers to. She should work longer hours and figure out her paperwork for herself.
d. Transfer to another department or quit her job. She clearly isn't cut out for this.

5

PLANNING FOR ACTION

Part A

1. What top five lessons have you learned about personal mastery while working through the book?
2. Starting now, what specific actions will you take to develop your personal mastery? To help others develop their personal mastery?

DEVELOPING PERSONAL MASTERY

Part B

Choose three of the seven personal mastery skills (taking responsibility; building emotional resilience; demonstrating a positive attitude; building confidence and competence; being conscientiousness and adaptable).

For each skill, think of a time when you struggled to exemplify it in your thoughts or actions.

1. Describe the situation (context, who was involved, who did what, what you did, etc.).
2. What rationale or reason did you give for what you did?
3. Looking back, how do you feel about your behavior?
4. What would you do differently if you could turn back the hands of time? (Review the descriptions of the personal mastery skills in the Introduction if you would like some hints.)

DEVELOPING PERSONAL MASTERY

About the Managerial Competencies Series

What's in the series?

This series is built around four managerial competency clusters: personal, people, purpose, and process.

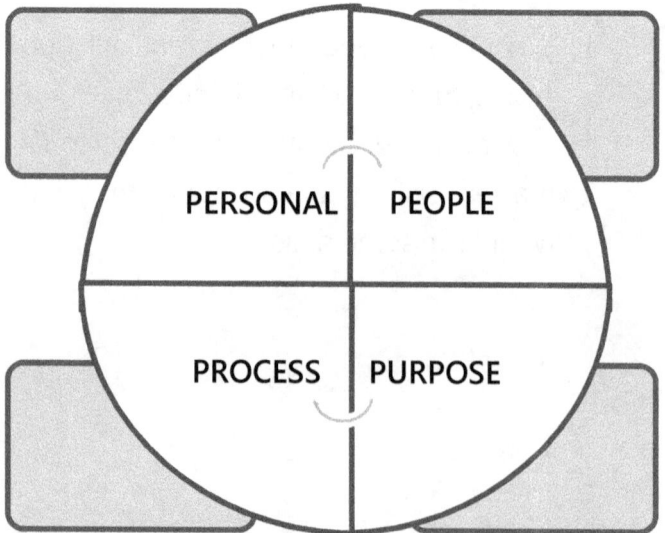

DEVELOPING PERSONAL MASTERY

Each cluster is made up of several competencies possessed by awesome managers. The series addresses a total of 15 competencies, each of which is the topic of a book of around 100 pages. Let's look at each cluster one at a time.

Personal Competencies

The starting point of the series is developing personal skills, given that effective self-management is essential for managing people, programs, and processes. It goes without saying that to manage others, you first must be able to manage yourself. People who are familiar with their personal strengths and challenges and who engage in effective self-management tend to work well with others.

DEVELOPING PERSONAL MASTERY

Here are the competencies included in the Personal Competencies cluster:

1. **Living the Core Values**, which involves demonstrating honesty, truthfulness, trustworthiness, reliability, fairness, and ethicality in all your decisions and interactions.
2. **Developing Personal Mastery** through personal responsibility, emotional resilience, constructive attitudes, self-confidence, adaptability, conscientiousness, and competence.
3. **Organizing Yourself** by focusing on your priorities and making effective use of time.

DEVELOPING PERSONAL MASTERY

4. **Building Stress Resilience**, which deals with managing life's stresses by developing personal hardiness.

People Competencies

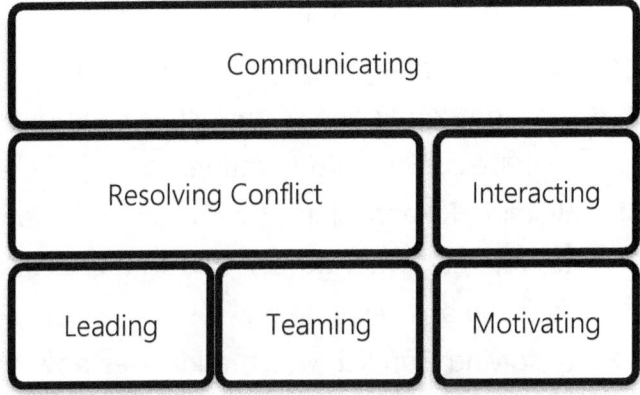

This cluster helps you examine and build your skills in working with and managing others. Although it's important for managers to be *technically* competent in order to gain credibility, interpersonal skills make the difference between awesome and not-so-awesome managers.

DEVELOPING PERSONAL MASTERY

The competencies included in the People Competencies cluster are:

5. **Communicating in Writing and through Presentations**, which focuses on communicating ideas effectively, whether verbally or in writing.
6. **Creating Engagement**, creating motivating working conditions so that staff contribute their best to the organization.
7. **Building Relationships**, which considers how to interact with others through effective listening and responding.
8. **Resolving Conflict**, which addresses how to deal with conflict in a productive manner.
9. **Leading Your Team**, which means leading in a manner that is appropriate for the needs of the situation and your team.
10. **Cultivating Team Spirit** by building a cohesive, high-performing team.

DEVELOPING PERSONAL MASTERY

Purpose and Process Competencies

This final cluster combines two sets of competencies. Purpose competencies offer you a "big picture" perspective of your organization and your own role in the organization. Process competencies help you translate this "big picture" (the *whats*) into everyday practice (the *hows*). In other words, they allow you to consider how work should be done as a means of accomplishing the goals of your organization and your work unit.

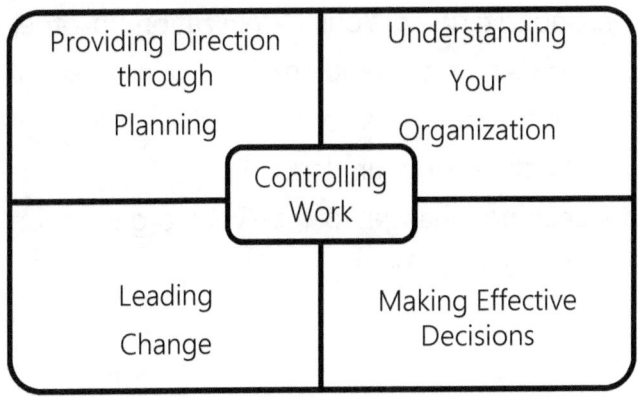

DEVELOPING PERSONAL MASTERY

Purpose and Process competencies include:

11. **Making Effective Decisions**, whether individually or in a team setting.
12. **Controlling Work Performance** by establishing control mechanisms to ensure results.
13. **Providing Direction through Planning**, which discusses the management process and offers tips for setting organizational direction and developing operational plans that fit this direction.
14. **Understanding Your Organization**, in other words, understanding the principles of organizing work and creating the right structure for your work unit.
15. **Leading Change** so that your organization and team thrive.

DEVELOPING PERSONAL MASTERY

How is each book organized?

Each book is organized according to a five-step learning process. This process is designed to help you learn in an active and reflective manner.

In each book, after a brief introduction, we jump right into the "**reality check.**" This series of self-coaching questions is meant to help you reflect on and develop insight into your own strengths and weaknesses in relation to a particular competence and, hopefully, motivate you to work on building your competencies.

DEVELOPING PERSONAL MASTERY

The reality check consists of the kinds of questions that management coaches might ask you, but that you can simply ask yourself. Just be sure to give yourself a chance to answer them!

Management coaches help managers view and understand situations from a variety of perspectives. But, if the art of coaching is asking challenging questions (as management coach Chantal Binet says), why not ask yourself these questions?

Second, to accompany you on your learning journey, you're offered a curated collection of **inspirational quotes**. There's lots of wisdom available from people from all walks of life. The quotes that grab us and speak to us do so because they have touched a nerve in us. They resonate with us, perhaps because they offer a message that we need to hear to continue developing or because they challenge us to become better people.

Third, we offer you tons of **tips and tricks** of awesome managers. These practical tips cover a gamut of perspectives and actions

DEVELOPING PERSONAL MASTERY

that you can take to improve your competencies. Ideally, they will encourage you to consider the variety of possibilities and alternatives that are available to you. It's up to you to decide which are the most useful to you. As you read this section, be sure to note or highlight the tips that stand out for you.

Next, we present a series of **dilemmas** or situations for you to resolve. This section will help you see how you might apply the tips and tricks from the previous section. We ask you to read the situation and then identify what you would do in these situations. You might choose one of the alternatives that is offered, or you might come up with your own creative solution. Ultimately, there are many factors and perspectives that might influence what is the "best" choice.

Finally, we nudge you to develop an **action plan** that you will *actually* implement. Developing and implementing an action plan is an especially important step because it helps you draw value from your efforts in working through this series. After all, you're reading this

DEVELOPING PERSONAL MASTERY

book because you're hoping to become an awesome manager, right? This means developing a realistic plan that describes the actions that you intend to take to become an awesome manager, implementing your plan, reflecting on how well it worked, and then continuously making any adjustments that are needed. So, the cycle starts again!

DEVELOPING PERSONAL MASTERY

How can you get the most out of the series?

You can read one or two books per month for an entire year, creating and implementing action plans for each book. Ultimately, this will help you develop a better understanding of yourself as a manager, your expectations, your strengths, and your areas for improvement.

As a way of refreshing your competencies, you can even re-read the books and re-visit your action plans in the future. Depending on what's happening in your life (new job, new team, new challenges), every time you read these books, you may develop new insights that help you deal with a situation.

DEVELOPING PERSONAL MASTERY

The knowledge of the world is only to be acquired in the world, and not in a closet.
Lord Chesterfield

What we have to learn to do,
we learn by doing.
Aristotle

Life is a succession of lessons which must be lived to be understood.
Ralph Waldo Emerson

What do this British statesman from the 1600s, Greek philosopher from 384 B.C., and American poet from the 1800s have in common? They all agree that learning comes from trying new things, not from simply sitting back and reading a book.

Don't just read the books; *do* them! Just reading the books won't transform you into an awesome manager. If you just read the books, you might get to know a lot about what it means to be an awesome manager without changing what you do in the workplace. How

DEVELOPING PERSONAL MASTERY

useful is that? Just like learning to ride a bike, it's impossible to develop your skills by simply reading or even thinking about what you have read. Besides, as *The Matrix* reminds us, "There's a difference between knowing the path and walking it."

In order to truly learn from our experiences, we need to do a complete loop of the learning cycle: we need to reflect on our experiences, figure out what lessons we learned, consider ways to apply these lessons, and then apply them. You may know people who seem to repeat the same mistakes over and over again or people who continually approach situations in a manner that doesn't work for them. It's probably because they go through life without taking the time to reflect, consider what they've learned, and develop an action plan in order to change their experiences. They're stuck somewhere on the learning cycle. David Kolb, the creator of this learning cycle, says that we all have a favorite place on the cycle where we tend to get stuck.

DEVELOPING PERSONAL MASTERY

Some people simply enjoy reading the books and reflecting on how they may relate to their lives, hopefully finding an opportunity to make use of their learning at some point in the future. However, without specific goals and action plans, they're not extracting as much value as they could from their investment of time and money.

Although this is partly due to differences in learning styles, it's also due to a reluctance to try something new and different. This may be caused by a fear of stepping out of one's comfort zone: what is familiar is comfortable. It may also be caused by a desire to accumulate a truckload of knowledge or have the perfect circumstances, such as the ideal boss or set of employees, before acting. Some of us think and think and continue to think without taking action. That used to be my personal downfall until I realized that knowing lots about a topic isn't the same as learning or making a difference in real life!

DEVELOPING PERSONAL MASTERY

At the other extreme, some of us take action without first reflecting on our experiences and what we learned from them. Some people prefer to go ahead and try things out right away. They're more action-oriented than their reflective counterparts. These folks typically find it especially challenging to slow down, consciously reflect on what they're reading, and develop a well thought out action plan before acting. In the same way, if you just read the books and do nothing else, the learning process will get stuck right off the bat.

Reflecting and taking action is the best solution. It's not enough to *know* how to do something. Although it's helpful and important to take the time to reflect and develop insights, at some point, you need to *do* the work yourself. Otherwise, as management expert Peter Block has said, "Waiting becomes an excuse for not acting."

Here are **five other important things** to do to maximize your learning. First, **keep a learning journal**. Record your thoughts as you read the books, answer the self-coaching

DEVELOPING PERSONAL MASTERY

questions, and develop your action plans. It will help you clarify your thinking, see patterns in what you have been experiencing and writing, and serve as a record of commitments you have made to yourself through your action plans. You'll be able to look back at what you've written and be impressed with all that you've learned! You could use a notebook or create an electronic document. Some people even email journal entries to themselves as a way of recording the day and time of their entries.

Second, **pull together a feedback team** who can help you get the most from this series. Your feedback team could be a group of four or five people that you have confidence in, such as coworkers, your manager, friends, and family members. Don't be shy about asking people for their support in helping you become a better manager; they are more willing to help you than you might think! These discussions will offer you different perspectives and exponentially increase how much you learn from the series. Besides, awesome

DEVELOPING PERSONAL MASTERY

managers surround themselves with people they trust who are willing to give them honest feedback that will help them grow as individuals.

In supporting you, others can play one or more of the following roles:

→ The Head: These people can help you analyze a question or problem objectively. They can sketch out options, compare data, or simply provide you with accurate information.

→ The Heart: These people can help you express your emotions and understand them better. They listen, cheer you up, don't make judgments, and give you a sense of security.

→ The Legs/Arms: These people help you do things. They go places with you; they make you get moving when you don't feel like it. These people energize you.

How can your manager help? Can your manager provide feedback, advice and tips, and time to complete the series? What will you

DEVELOPING PERSONAL MASTERY

do to get your manager's help? For example, could you meet with your manager once every two weeks to discuss your progress and talk about how to manage effectively?

How can your peers help? Can your peers provide feedback, tips about managing, or coaching when needed? What will you do to get their help? Could you schedule a coffee break with them once every two weeks to discuss what you're learning and to share tips? Can you work through the series together?

How can your employees help? Can your employees provide feedback regarding your strengths and opportunities for improvement or work with you to develop a plan for making your unit function more effectively? What will you do to get their help? Could you meet with them once every two weeks to discuss what you're learning and how your team can implement elements of your action plan?

How can your friends help? Could they provide feedback, tips about managing, and encouragement for you to try new things?

DEVELOPING PERSONAL MASTERY

What will you do to get their help? Could you organize a dinner with them once every two weeks to discuss what you're learning and how to implement your action plan?

Third, **develop and implement a SMARTER action plan.** You know you've really learned something when your behavior changes (for the better, of course). Insights and tips that are meaningful to you will change your perspective *and* your behaviors. That's why each book ends by inviting you to develop an action plan. Your plan should be **Specific, Measurable, Attainable, Realistic, Timely, Exciting, and Rewarded.** Think about things that you need to start doing, stop doing, or continue doing. Here's an example: "By the end of next week, I will write two letters – one to my former manager and one to my best friend – expressing my gratitude for their coaching and willingness to challenge me to

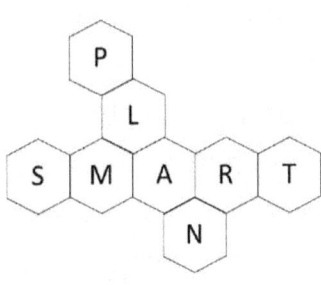

DEVELOPING PERSONAL MASTERY

become a better person. I will send these letters by email no later than Friday afternoon." Write your action plan in your journal. Revisit it to check your progress, and revise your plan as needed. Remember to ask for help from others, evaluate your progress, and reward yourself for your progress toward becoming an awesome manager.

Fourth, **identify obstacles or barriers that might get in your way of making the most of the series** and implementing your action plans; for example, lack of time or energy, poor personal habits, others' expectations, etc. List these in the column labelled "Obstacles" on the following page. Now, think about specific actions that you can take to address them and place these in the "Neutralizers" column; for example, meet with your manager, plan small wins or ways to celebrate your progress, etc.

DEVELOPING PERSONAL MASTERY

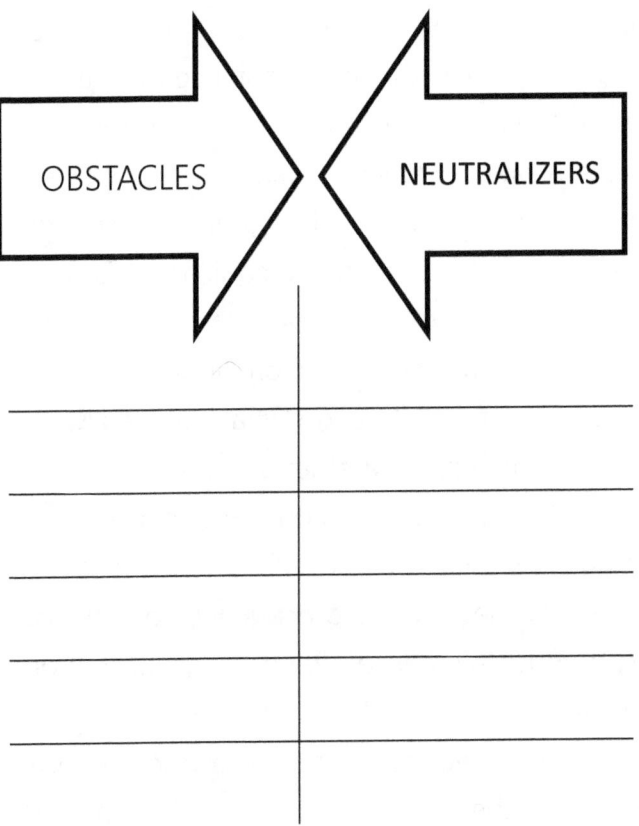

Finally, **do what you need to do to motivate yourself.** Don't wait to be motivated to get started. Instead, get started, and motivation will come knocking at your door!

DEVELOPING PERSONAL MASTERY

Also, try to be comfortable with discomfort. As you change how you manage, you may meet with some resistance from those around you. You exist in a system of relationships. Because systems are geared toward equilibrium (stability), if you change one thing in the system, the equilibrium is shot, and the system is upset. There may be pressure from others and from your own sense of comfort for you to do what you've always done regardless of whether or not it works.

It may be tempting to give up when things feel unnatural, but rest assured that this is part of the learning process. It's normal that trying out new ways of doing things makes you feel a bit uncomfortable in one way or another. Sometimes, we come across awesome folks who do their work without hesitation and seemingly without effort. It's easy to forget that they've gone through the highs and lows of the learning process. For example, think of Cirque du Soleil acrobats who seem to perform stunts with ease and pinpoint accuracy. It took them lots of practice, repetition, and even

DEVELOPING PERSONAL MASTERY

occasional failures to get to that skill level. Experts make things look easy.

Are you ready to begin your awesome journey? Earl Nightingale once said, "All you need is the plan, the road map, and the courage to press on to your destination." I hope that this series serves as your guide and road map on your journey toward awesomeness.

REFERENCES

Burns, D. D. (2009). *Feeling Good: The New Mood Therapy*. New York: Harper.

Chismar, D. (2001). Vice and virtue in everyday life. *Journal of Business Ethics*, 29, 169-176.

Covey, S. (1998). *The 7 Habits of Highly Effective People*. Provo, UT: Franklin Covey.

Dweck, C. S. (2006). *Mindset: The New Psychology of Success*. Random House Incorporated.

Dyer, W. (1978). *Pulling your own Strings*. New York: Harper Perennial.

Ekman, P. (1973). Cross-cultural studies of facial express. In P. Ekman (Ed.). *Darwin and Facial Expression* (pp. 169-222). New York: Academic Press.

Ellis, A. (1957). Rational Psychotherapy and Individual Psychology. *Journal of Individual Psychology*, 13: 38-44.

Fletcher, B. (1992) *50 Activities for Achieving Change*. HRD Press, Inc.

Hughes, R., Ginnett, R., & Curphy, G. (2011). *Leadership: Enhancing the Lessons of Experience*. Boston: McGraw-ill Irwin.

Karpman, S. (1968). Fairy tales and script drama analysis. *Transactional Analysis Bulletin,* 26 (7) 39 – 43.

Luhn, R. R. (1992). *Managing Anger. Methods for a Happier and Healthier Life*. United States of America: Crisp Publications, Inc.

Neidhardt, J., et al. (1985). *Managing Stress: A Complete Self-Help Guide*. Vancouver, BC: International Self-Counsel Press.

Robinson, J. (1982). *Stress and How to Live with it*. Des Moines: Meredith Corp.

Steinmetz, J. (1980). *Managing Stress before it Manages You*. Palo Alto, CA: Bull Pub. Co.

DEVELOPING PERSONAL MASTERY

Playbooks in the Managerial Competencies Series

1. Living the Core Values
2. Developing Personal Mastery
3. Organizing Yourself
4. Building Stress Resilience
5. Communicating in Writing and through Presentations
6. Creating Engagement
7. Building Relationships
8. Resolving Conflict
9. Leading Your Team
10. Cultivating Team Spirit
11. Making Effective Decisions
12. Controlling Work Performance
13. Providing Direction through Planning
14. Understanding Your Organization
15. Leading Change

www.ingramcontent.com/pod-product-compliance
Lightning Source LLC
Chambersburg PA
CBHW070305230526
45470CB00002B/732